The Lively
ART of
INK PAINTING

The Lively ART of

INK PAINTING

By Ryozo Ogura

JAPAN PUBLICATIONS, INC., TOKYO

Published by Japan Publications, Inc., Tokyo

Distributed by Japan Publications Trading Company
1255 Howard St., San Francisco, Calif. 94103
175 Fifth Ave., New York, N.Y. 10010
Central P.O. Box 722, Tokyo

Library of Congress Catalog Card No. 68–19980

First printing: December 1968

Printed in Japan

Preface

Throughout the ages, man has chosen his favorite recreation such as sports, music, art, dancing, and others to suit his individual needs and gratify his feelings of creativity, however, I feel that no other pastime is as economical and enjoyable as sumi-e, which is Japanese brush painting. As one becomes more skilled in sumi-e, much enjoyment and spiritual uplifting is attained.

Although many traditionalists feel that an understanding and insight into Zen Buddhism and Oriental philosophy is important to the ultimate success in orthodox sumi-e, my aim in this book is not to delve into the phylosophical aspects of this ancient art, but rather to create a desire in the individual to study this type of painting for his own pleasure and gratification. I hope to achieve this goal by showing techniques of painting familiar subjects, and in this way infuse freshness into an ancient style.

I should like to take this opportunity to thank Reverend Gyoko Saito, Mr. Paul Shimokubo, my daughter Donna Ogura, and the photographer Mr. Ray Akins. Without the kind help of these people this book might never have been written.

R.O.

5

Contents

Introduction

The apparent simplicity of sumi-e, pictures of one subject done in shades of black on white paper, is very deceptive. To achieve the desired effect, the artist must master the technique of shading within a single brush stroke to suggest, in monochrome black, a whole spectrum of colors. Doing this requires him to prepare himself mentally and physically before he picks up his brush. He must be able to visualize textures, shapes, and colors, and attune his whole body to the painting process. By hinting at depth and surface with a minimum of effort, he must reveal the essential differences between subjects as varied as a downy, fluffy chick or a black, gnarled plum bough. A few strokes must give life, though not necessarily realism, to what he paints. Just as a modern poet may not be fettered by conventional English grammar, so the sumi-e artist is free of the limitations of exact representation. Though his task is not easy, if the artist is successful, the viewer will, upon reflection, feel what is intended.

Ultimately, freedom of movement is the aim of the sumi-e painter, but paradoxically such freedom comes only from strict discipline and control. Consequently, an accomplished sumi-e artist, seemingly able to dash off a fine picture in three minutes, has actually spent many years developing speed and cultivating the skill required in making every stroke neat, clean, and as near perfect as possible. After all, sumi-e, like life, does not permit the eradication of errors.

A Brief Outline of Japanese Painting

The overwhelming influence of Buddhism (traditionally said to have entered Japan in 552) during the Asuka and Nara periods (552–784) inspired great artistic activity, the relics of which, though mostly sculpture, include a few paintings: the pictures on the Tamamushi and Tachibana Shrines in the temple Horyu-ji, in Nara and the frescoes (now seriously damaged by fire and water) on the walls of the Main Hall of the same temple. As is to be expected, Chinese and Korean influences underlie all of these works; indeed, the frescoes occupy an almost unique position in Oriental art because they represent the glory of Chinese painting in the first full flush of the mature T'ang dynasty.

In the Heian period (784–1185), the importation of esoteric Buddhist sects – Shingon and Tendai, both more popular in appeal than the involved theologies prominent in the earlier years – stimulated a great demand for Buddhist pictures, particularly mandara, or graphic representations of often extremely complex religious concepts. In these, and in many other phases of the art of the period, Chinese influence continued strong, but the Japanese were at the same time developing a form of secular painting that better expressed their own national feelings and aesthetic tendencies. These were the *yamato-e,* best exemplified by such narrative picture scrolls, representing static scenes in rich gold and color masses with luxurious attention to details of costume and setting, as the famous *Tale of Genji* and the *Diary of Murasaki Shikibu.* The satirical *Animal Caricatures,* lighter in feeling and painted with a more active line and less color, represent still another interesting application of the scroll method. This true Japanese artistic tradition of painting continued to evolve during the Kamakura period (1192–1333) while foreign influences waned.

After the collapse of the T'ang, relationships between Japan and China chilled till they reached a nadir with the attempted invasions of Japanese shores by the hordes of Kublai Khan in

1274 and again in 1281. However, in the Muromachi period (1336–1573), ties were renewed, this time with the Ming, and Japanese monks and artists traveled to China to learn the ink-painting styles of Zen, the contemplative Buddhist sect, introduced into Japan during the Kamakura period, when military feudal barons found its anti-intellectualism appealing. Many great painters in the tradition produced powerful black and white paintings in the manner of Chinese Zen painters, and later, in the seventeenth century, another painter, Miyamoto Musashi (or Niten, as he is also known) was to make the style even more masculine.

The greatest painter of this period of revived Chinese tendencies was the priest-monk Sesshu, who made a trip to China to study but found that few of the Ming artists then active were his equal. Sesshu's greatest contribution was the development of a truly Japanese manner within the framework of Chinese material.

Followers in the Chinese trend, but also definitely Japanese in manner, were Kano Masanobu and his son Motonobu, the founders of what must surely be one of the most brilliant art families in the world.

The descendants of the two first Kano painted the countless screens and sliding panels that glorified the castles built during the turbulent Momoyama period (1573–1615). After the first founders of the house had succeeded in nationalizing the Chinese styles current in their day, the following generations carefully adhered to safe, traditional contents. So well did their work embody the Confucian ethics on which the government of the Tokugawa period (1615–1867) was built, that the rulers appointed the Kano their artistic mouthpieces. After this, the school lost its vitality and degenerated into slick professionalism.

The Tosa School, originally staunch supporters of native Japanese elements in art and the painters of colorful scrolls for the Imperial court, gradually fell under the shadow of the official Kano, until they lost importance and identity. Later, another bearer of the Tosa name was to reestablish the school prestige but, ironically, through paintings of a Chinese, rather than a Japanese, nature.

As the official painters lapsed into stale orthodoxy, a new group of artists, headed by Sotatsu and Korin, arose once again to give expression to the true Japanese fondness for flat color and decorative forms. These men provided ornamentation for the homes of the growing wealthy merchant class as the Sinicized painters of the Kano had done earlier for the castle builders.

In the eighteenth century, Maruyama Okyo established an important line of painting theory combining the Kano theme, with intense naturalism. His style, though different from the deliberately ornamental approach of Korin and Sotatsu, is no less Japanese.

During the eighteenth century, a group of scholars and poets devoted themselves to the landscape ink styles of the Southern school of Sung painters and produced many exquisite works.

In general, as the Tokugawa government grew old and fell on hard times, in the eighteenth and nineteenth centuries, painting began to stagnate, but one group of artists did brighten the last years of the period of national isolation. These men were the designers of *ukiyo-e,* whose intention was to return to Japanese traditions of color and form, but who succeeded in doing much more. They were the first Japanese artists to produce extensive portrayals of the lives of the ordinary people, and their popularity was, accordingly, immense.

Implements

The accompanying photograph shows the materials used for sumi-e painting. Though substitution is possible for some of them, brushes, inkstone, paper, and ink should be of Oriental manufacture. Naturally, poor tools are unsuitable, but it is also unwise to pay extremely high prices for materials. The best way to make progress is to accustom yourself to one particular kind of brush, ink, and paper.

INKSTONE

Japanese inkstones, *suzuri,* are made from various materials, but those of real stone are the

---

Essential sumi-e equipment: inkstone, ink stick, brushes, dish for washing brushes, water container, porcelain dishes for thinning ink, shaping brush points, and testing ink color values.

best. Chinese inkstones, *tankei*, particularly prized by sumi-e artists in Japan, have a dense composition that produces smooth, practically non-absorbent surfaces, which stay wet for a long time. Some inkstones are rectangular and some round, but the former is the usual type.

BRUSHES

Bamboo-handled sumi-e brushes use a number of different kinds of long or short, soft or hard animal hairs. In the center of the brush are hard, water resistant bristles, taken from the areas near the hoofs of horses or deer. The periphery uses very soft bristles, and between the two extremes are hairs of moderate texture. The hard central bristles permit fine black lines, whereas the softer ones produce gentle, rounded strokes. Since brushes of all sizes above medium contain a paste stiffener, pressing too hard on them sometimes

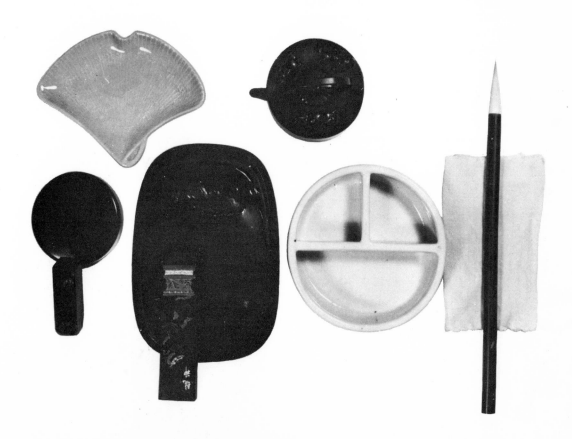

causes the bristles to drop out. It is, therefore, a good idea to soften a new brush in water for about five or six minutes and dry it thoroughly before using it in ink. Avoid hot water, and when using or washing brushes do not press hard because the bristles are simply tied with string and held in place at the end of the bamboo handle with fish glue.

A good brush, whether its bristles are horse, deer, cow, fox, or badger, must be resilient and must take ink well.

The lack of close detail in sumi-e makes extremely fine brushes unnecessary except for such special purposes as painting human faces.

The most important of all sumi-e tools, the brush, deserves both careful selection and good care. After use, it should always be washed and hung up to dry. Many brushes come with cords for hanging; those without them should be properly fitted immediately.

PAPER

Generally Chinese or Japanese papers are used for sumi-e because their textures and colors best reveal the subtle tonal changes of *notan*, the light and dark shading of ink. Western papers or any papers with sizing are totally unsuitable. The differences in color and absorption power of the various kinds of paper, naturally, produce dif-

ferent effects in the sumi-e. The beginner must remember that poor quality paper, brushes, and ink, by making it difficult to achieve the desired result, frustrate rather than encourage. Good materials, therefore, are of paramount importance.

INK

Sumi-e inks are a compound of a fish-base glue, called *nikawa,* and the soot obtained from the smoke of burning pine. Kneaded and poured into forms, this mixture is allowed to dry for about four months. Of the three tones of ink— pure black, bluish, and brownish— specialists usually prefer the bluish variety, and even when using pure black they avoid excessively dark varieties. Some say that Chinese inks improve in quality with age. Cheap inks will lack the perfume used in better grades, and some varieties even contain stone particles which damage the inkstone; these should be carefully avoided. A bad ink stick—one containing sand— will make a grating sound when rubbed on the inkstone.

In addition to these implements, a container for water to wash the brushes, a mat called a *mosen* or a few layers of flannel to put under the paper when you paint, and small dishes for blending ink are necessary.

Various ink sticks and inkstones.

Brushes.

15

Holding and Using the Brush

The proper way to hold the brush (Fig. 1) is with the thumb, index, middle and fourth fingers, the last serving as the main support point. Gripping the brush too tightly makes proper movement impossible. Only with progress, after you come to regard the brush as an extension of your fingers and when your spirit and body are so unified that you paint with your whole arm or whole body, will you understand truly correct brush use. Nonetheless, learning not to use your wrist alone is a good first step. To charge the brush with ink (Fig. 2), first fill it thoroughly; then correct its shape and even the distribution of ink among the bristles by pulling it on the higher part of the ink stone. Next, using a small flat dish, check the shading of the ink in the brush (Fig. 3).

Before I begin the basics of brush use, I want to emphasize an important point. Never attempt to move your brush in a direction opposite to the lay of the bristles. For instance, in Fig. 4, the bristles point in direction A making it impossible to paint in that direction, though directions B, C, and D present no difficulties. In Fig. 5, you must avoid directions A and B. These examples concern instances in which the brush is held nearly parallel to the surface of the paper. Another movement for a different holding angle is shown in Fig. 6; and Fig. 7 shows yet another in which the brush, inclined more than in Fig. 6, produces a very wide line. The angle in Fig. 8 is nearly the same as that in Fig. 7, but the brush inclines in the opposite direction. The angle in Fig. 9 is the opposite of that in Fig. 4; Fig. 10 shows the proper way to hold the brush nearly perpendicular to the paper.

Clearly revealing the directions of the brush points, the lines in Figs. 11 and 12 suggest the trunks of trees. Fig. 13 shows the basic way to paint a round dot, whereas, Fig. 14 shows a way to suggest the body of a fish by using the brush stroke in Fig. 5.

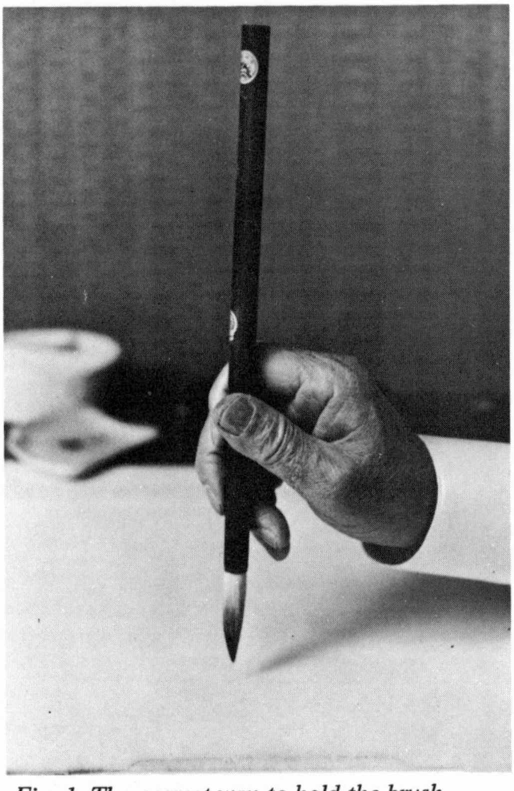

Fig. 1. The correct way to hold the brush.

Fig. 2. Removing excess ink and shaping the tip of the brush.
Fig. 3. Checking tonal values and the amount of ink in the brush.

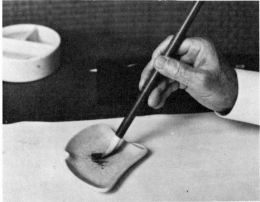

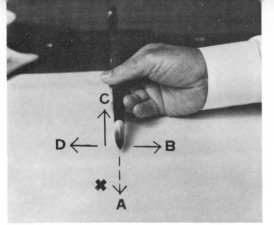

Fig. 4

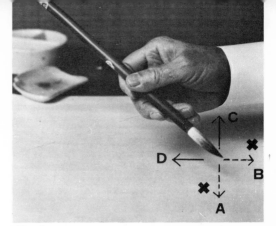

Fig. 5

Fig. 6

Fig. 7

Fig. 8

Fig. 9

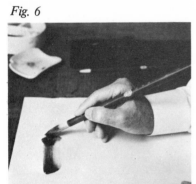

Fig. 10

Fig. 11

Fig. 12

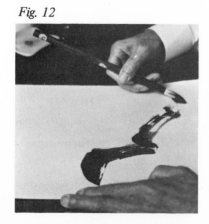

Fig. 13

Fig. 14

Ink Shading

DARK INK

Though, by definition, darker than the medium and light shades, rather than cover an area with dense uniform black, dark ink should contain a certain amount of vibrant shading to avoid seeming flat and dead.

MEDIUM INK

After washing the brush and removing the excess moisture from its bristles with a cloth, dip the end in dark ink, and move the brush around in a circular movement on the surface of a small porcelain dish until the ink blends throughout the bristles to a medium darkness.

LIGHT INK

Once again, wash the brush, but leave a certain amount of moisture in the bristles. This time, dip the tip in the medium ink remaining on the porcelain dish, and making circular motions, blend it till it is a light shade. It is convenient to make small amounts of each ink in separate dishes so that they are ready when you need them. Though all three shades run and blur, the light variety sometimes fades to near invisibility.

1. Dark Ink

2. Medium Ink

3. Light Ink

Three-ink Stroke

To paint one stroke containing a harmonious shading of all three-ink shades, first wash the brush in clear water. After charging it full with light ink, dip it to about two-thirds its length in medium, and finally about one-third in dark ink. One stroke with a brush so filled produces the full spectrum of ink colors.

FISH BODIES

Simplicity is often the key to success, as this method of painting a fish body suggests. Charge the brush as explained above, and make lines either from the top of the page downward or from the bottom upward. The shape of the line resembles the form of a fish. The three-ink shading simultaneously suggests the darker area along the fish's back, the whiter belly, and the medium area between.

BAMBOO STALK

Three-ink lines painted from the bottom upward suggest the round shape of a bamboo stalk. To give the effect of a light breeze, incline the lines; to paint a group of bamboo stalks, vary the intensity of the inks to indicate the spatial relations among the individual plants.

Begin with Familiar Subject Matter

Squirrel

1. Begin with the eye, then add the nose.
2. Holding the brush nearly parallel to the surface of the paper add the forward ear, sketch in the ear outline, and finally with a single stroke suggest the far ear. Strokes should always follow the directions indicated by the arrows.
3. The front paw should be rounded as if the squirrel were holding a chestnut.
4. Add the other front paw, and complete the hand, with a single stroke.
5. Paint the shoulders.
6. Indicate the rounded back with two strokes.
7. Suggest general shape of the rear paws as you did the forepaws, except that in this case the toes must be straight.
8. Holding the brush nearly parallel to the surface of the paper and making as wide a line as possible, add the tail. Finish the squirrel by adding a chestnut between the front paws. With a few additional strokes, draw a branch for the squirrel to stand on.

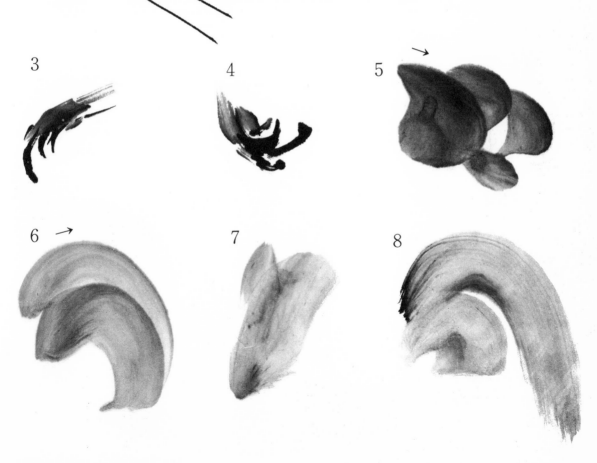

Mouse and Corn

1-9.   Horizontal strokes of the brush complete the shape of the ear of corn. Using one stroke to paint the mouse's head, add the ears; then change brushes, and with dark ink, paint the ear outlines. Two strokes of medium ink complete the mouse's body. Continue the upper stroke to make the tail. Wait until the ink is thoroughly dry to add dark eyes, claws, nose, and whiskers. All of the corn kernels in a single row must be the same shade. The cherries on the side of the picture provide balance to the composition. Instead of portraying the corn silk with several thin lines, use one or two broad ones.

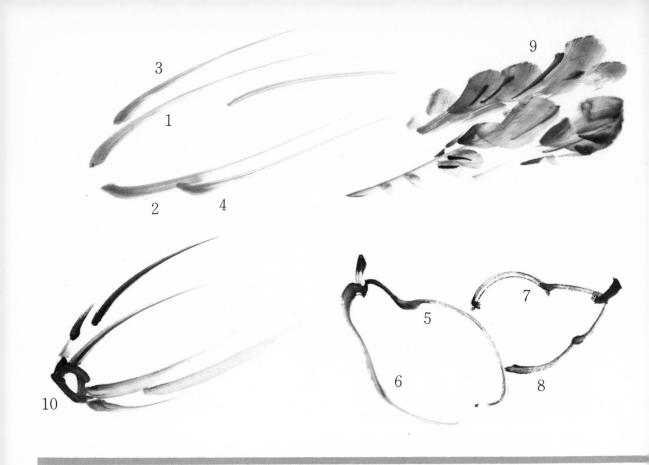

Chinese Cabbage and Pears

First, using medium ink draw lines 1,2,3, and 4 fast enough to prevent blurring. Next make the pear shapes with lines 5, 6, 7, and 8 and the leaves with 9. Wash the brush, and after charging it with light and medium inks, shade the pear with broad upward strokes following lines 6 and 8. With dark ink, stroke in the calyx at the bottom of the pear in the foreground and the base of the cabbage stalk.

I use this combination of vegetables and fruit because they make an interesting composition. Both Chinese cabbage and pears occur frequently in sumi-e.

Chinese Bellflower

Wild Rose

After painting 1, 2 and 3 in downward, slanting medium-ink strokes, wash the brush and add 4, 5, and 6 in light ink; then add 7, 8 and leaves 9 and 10. Paint the stems (11 and 12) in upward lines. Use medium ink for leaf 13, but change to light ink for 14, 15, and 16. Using dark ink, finish the picture by adding the rose stamens, the veins of the leaves, and some thorns.

Cherries and a Basket of Strawberries

Using light ink for the shape and dark ink for the calyx paint a strawberry as in Fig. 1. Adding the achenes with medium ink, produce a picture like those in 2 and 3. Sketch in the general form of the basket with dark ink: 4, 5, 6, and 7. Wash the brush, and use light ink to suggest perspective on the sides. Avoiding perfect circles, draw three cherries, their stems, and two leaves. Shade them with light ink.

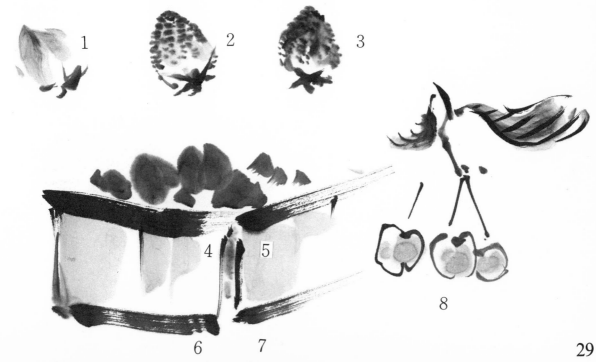

1   2   3

4   5

6   7

8

Capturing the Liveliness of Insects and Frogs

Insects

Moving the brush as the arrows indicate, paint the four sections of the butterfly's wings, but leave space in the middle to paint the darker body. The angles of the antennae suggest that the butterfly is flying

The praying mantis (2) and the katydids (4) and (5) employ similar brushwork, but the forelegs of the mantis should suggest great strength and the position that gives it its name.

In the dragonfly (3), draw the brush horizontally from the outside inward, and leave space between the sets of wings to paint the body and head in darker ink.

With the katydids, too, first paint the wings and then the head and legs. Ordinarily, it is necessary to paint the legs of only one side.

Paint the transparent wings of the bees (6) with light ink.

With most insects it is important to draw clearly separated head, breast, and abdomen sections and to indicate three pairs of legs; however, in the case of spiders, four pairs of legs, but no abdomen section, are needed. In keeping with traditional Japanese classifications, I have included the snail (7) among the insects.

Insect Cage and Katydid

Frogs

The following is the order of parts in painting the frog:
head, mouth, back, legs, and paws. For the top of the
mushroom on which the frog sits, charge a brush with
medium and dark inks, and work from the left. Dark ink
for the outline and light ink for the shading produce the
effect of the stem of the mushroom.

It is a good idea to observe frogs and to practice
painting them in many postures.

Traditional Sumi-e Trees and Flowers

Branches, Trees, and Flowers

Dots made with the tip of the brush can represent groupings of leaves or trees (Fig. 1). Fig. 2 shows how lines made by drawing the tip of the brush downward can serve the same function. The horizontal lines in Fig. 3 suggest evergreens, whereas the lines in Fig. 4 represent broadleaf trees like the maple. Suggesting distant foliage is accomplished with narrow horizontal lines (Fig. 5): distant mountains, with horizontal lines like those in Fig. 6. Groups of narrow, upward lines (Fig. 7) become lawn, and dots grouped like those in Fig. 8, either small flowers or groups of large leaves seen from a distance.

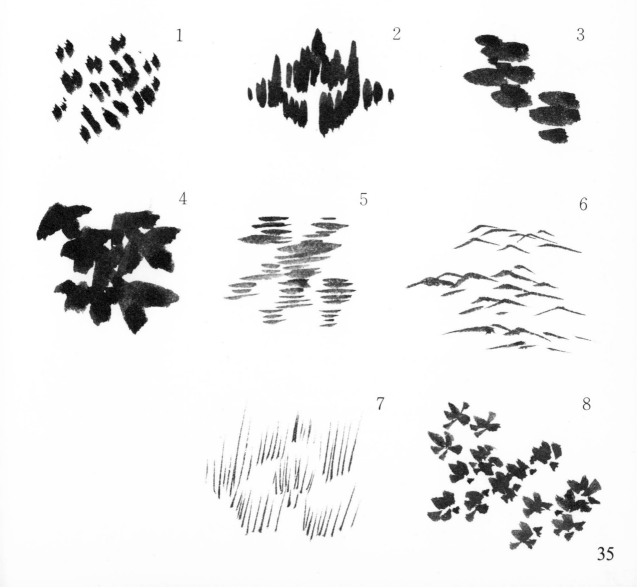

Curves and bends in lines can express a wide variety of leaf and branch types (Figs. 9—16).

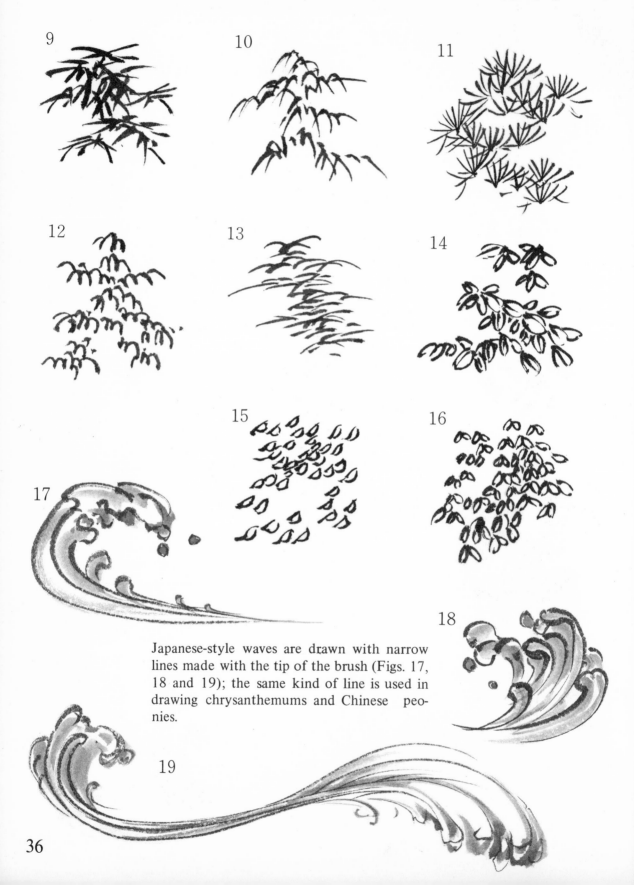

Japanese-style waves are drawn with narrow lines made with the tip of the brush (Figs. 17, 18 and 19); the same kind of line is used in drawing chrysanthemums and Chinese peonies.

Differences between the Results of Horizontal and Vertical Brushwork

Paint the leaves of the tree in Fig. A with horizontal strokes and the trunk and branches with downward vertical ones.

In Fig. B, the large trunk is painted in upward vertical lines (1, 2, 3, 4, and 5), but the smaller branches are downward strokes (6, 7, 8, and 9) executed with a lightness that evokes the feeling of a weeping willow.

To paint the forest, use dark ink, and holding the brush perpendicular to the paper, move it horizontally, stopping midway the stroke, and lifting it from the paper. Continue with line groups 2, 3, 4, and 5. Next, wash the brush, charge it with medium ink, shade the trees, and finally add the trunks by painting upward vertical lines.

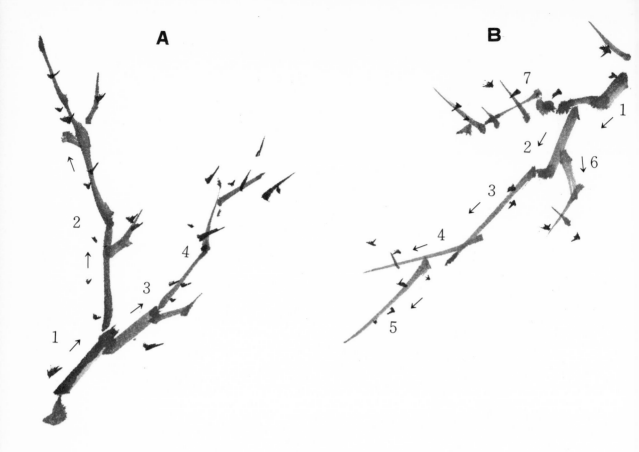

Painting Branches

The branch in Fig. A is made by constantly pressing the brush and making the upward lines shown by the arrows. Add the smaller twigs by making a number of dot-like lines.

Although the method used in the branch in Fig. B is essentially the same, the brush movement is downward.

Willow

First the trunk (1, 2, 3, 4, and 5) and the branches in disconnected groups, A, B, C, D, and E, then the young slender branches painted as the arrows indicate (6), and finally the pale-ink wash suggest the feeling of a willow. Alter the expression by directing the small branches to suggest a windy day.

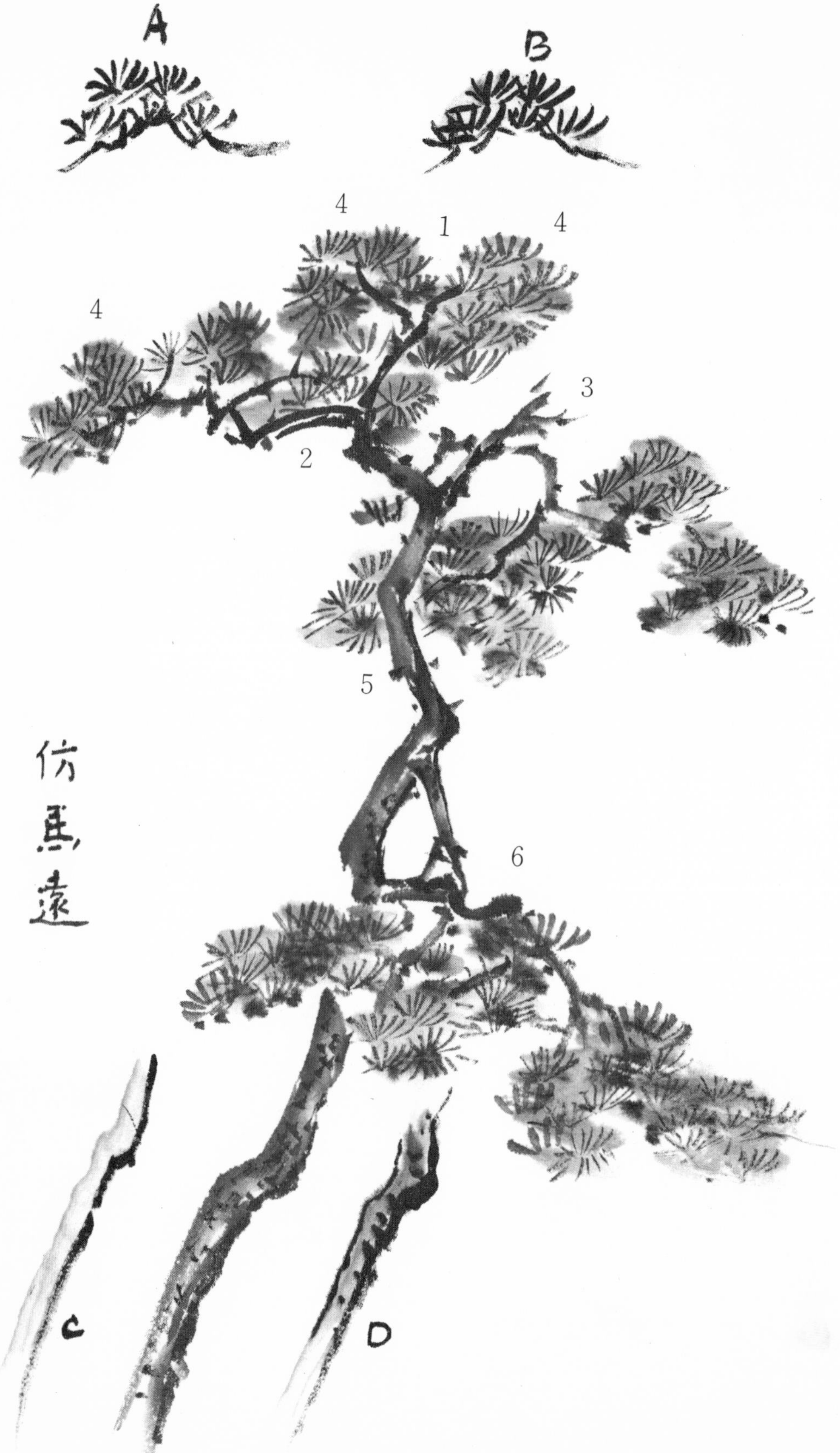
A
B
4
1
4
4
3
2
5
仿馬遠
6
C
D

Pine

Based on a painting by Maen, a famous Chinese
painter, this lovely pine is a fine model for beginners.
Although I do not know what brush stroke order Maen
used, the following will prove effective. First place the
branches as in 1, 2, and 3. Next, paint the leaves in 4,
and add the trunk (5). Continue with the branches in 6,
and add the leaves as in the upper section. Finally, give
the finishing touches to the lowest part of the trunk,
and shade the leaves with light ink. Figs. A and B show
how to paint and shade pine needless; C and D explain
the trunk. Details of pines, incidentally, are one of the
most beloved of sumi-e subjects.

Sumi-e Birds—
Quick Eye and
Firm Footing

Fledgling Sparrow

Begin with the sparrow, a bird known to everyone and particularly charming when only a fledgling. Paint the beak (1) with dark ink; then changing to a medium brush and charging it first with medium ink, then with a small amount of dark ink at the tip, hold the brush at an angle, and press it down to make the birds head. Using a similar press of the brush make the back (2) with a mark a little larger than the head. Quickly add the smaller mark on the right, and using two or three darker dots, sketch in the wings In the tail (3), avoid excessively strong lines or dark ink because the bird is not supposed to be full grown. Before painting the breast, dry the brush with a cloth. Try to give the impression of a well-fed young sparrow. Finally, for the foot, use a darker ink than that in the beak. All of the brush strokes in the fledgling sparrow are from left to right.

 1

 2

 3

4

5

Sparrow

The size and shape of the beak often determine bird classifications. In contract to the long, narrow beaks of insect-eating birds, those of seed-eaters—like the sparrow—should always be painted short, broad, and well set into the head. When the beak is finished (1), add the eye and the head, and sketch in the thinner lines of the breast. Using a dry brush, add the shoulder section (4), the tail (5), and the wings (6). After shaping the bird with slightly darker ink, use very dark ink for the feet. In this version, the sparrow is standing on a flat surface, not on a twig.

1

2

3

4

5

6

Various Bird Beaks

Three Sparrow Paintings

48

Kingfisher

The kingfishers, devourers of small fish, have long and relatively large beaks, distinctive topknots, and thick, large feet. They make their nests in hollows in cliffs. The best way to express their essential qualities is to keep in mind the image of a sharp-eyed bird on a branch over a river always poised for a lightning-quick swoop down on any fish that swims by.

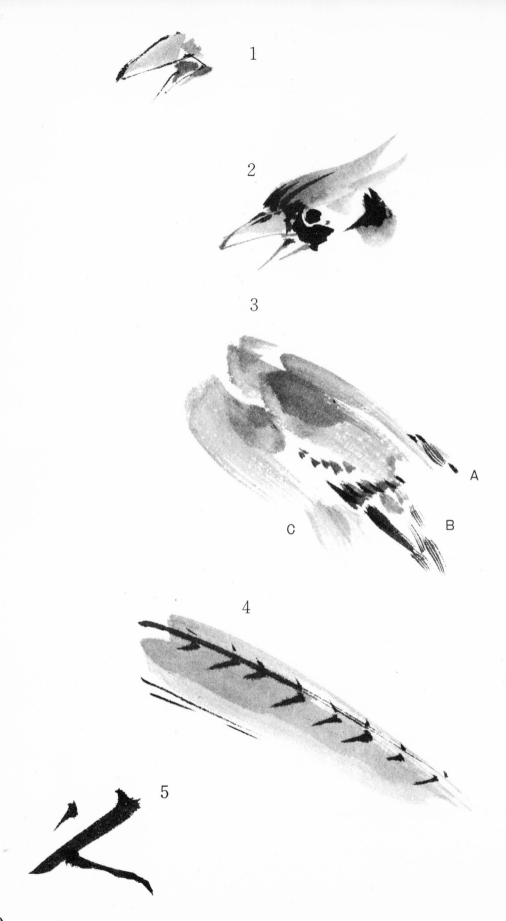

1

2

3

A

B

C

4

5

Blue Jay

Using light ink sketch in the surfaces of the open beak, and changing to a finer brush charged with dark ink, draw the beak outline. After brushing in the topknot with light ink, change to dark ink, and paint the eye and the dark areas around it, being careful to leave the white spaces indicated in 2. Making a white collar around the neck and using a brush filled with light ink, add the back section (3 A), then the wing (B) and the breast (C). Highlight the wings with darker ink. For the tail feathers, first use light ink; then indicate the stripes in the jay's tail (4) and foot (5) with dark ink.

Cormorant

Start with a small brush to make the shape of the beak, the cormorant's most distinctive feature, and after shading it as in 2, add the keen eye (3), and finally with a medium brush and dark ink, fill in the head. Wash the brush, and following the arrow, make a neck line (5), suggest the bird's full craw with the line in 6, and after dipping the tip of the brush in dark ink, paint the shoulder and back (7, 8). Use dark ink for the wing (9, 10), tail, and foot (11, 12). The foot must be placed in the center of the picture to give the impression of supporting the bird's entire weight. After sketching in the surface of the ground with light ink, add a few blades of grass in the background.

1

2

3

4

5

8 7

6

9

10

11

12

13

14

Cock

Steps 1 and 2 show how to use first a fine brush to paint the beak and eye and then a larger brush and darker ink for the comb, made with upward strokes. Downward strokes in 3 represent the wattles, and a finer downward line, the back of the neck. Medium ink is used around the eye and lighter ink for the breast. After making the lines of feathers in 4, using medium ink follow the arrows in 5, 6 to paint the tail. Highlight with dark ink.

To paint the legs, using a large brush and medium ink, press the brush to the paper to make the mark in 7; repeat for a similar, though smaller, mark to represent the leg on the far side of the body (8). Use dark ink to paint the visible parts of the lower legs (9, 10) so that they seem strong enough to support the weight of the whole body. Conceal the claws with grass.

1

2

3

4

5

6

7

8

9

10

Owl

First with a small brush and dark ink, paint the outline of the beak and the eye (1, 2); then changing to a medium brush and medium ink, color in the area around the eye—the red area on a real pheasant (2). Next, wash the brush, charge it with dark ink, and paint the comb and wattles (3). With dark ink and a medium brush, paint the A section of 4 in horizontal strokes from left to right. Follow the same procedure for the B section; then wash the brush, fill it with light ink, and paint the wing (C). For the tail in 5, wash a large brush thoroughly, fill it with medium ink, and dip the tip only in dark ink. After making the first long stroke of the tail, wash the brush, and soften the effect by adding the lines in 6.

The thigh section (4-D) requires a medium brush filled with medium ink. Next, add the lower section of the leg and the claw with dark ink (E).

This completes the general form of the body. Finish up by using a small brush and dark ink to add the stripes to the tail; then use medium ink for the mottling in the breast.

Instead of being too concerned with details, concentrate on total balance, and try to achieve the effect of a running pheasant.

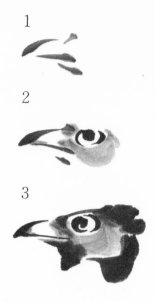

1

2

3

59

Flowers—Familiar and Always Popular

Crocus

The bud (1) is made with descending light-ink strokes, 2 is the open blossom, and 3, the entire flower. Picture 4 contains the stalk, and 5 and 6, the needle-like leaves.

Fig. A shows a half-open flower, B, a blossom in full bloom, and C, a blossom and bud.

People in cold climates love the brave crocus as a harbinger of spring.

A

B

C

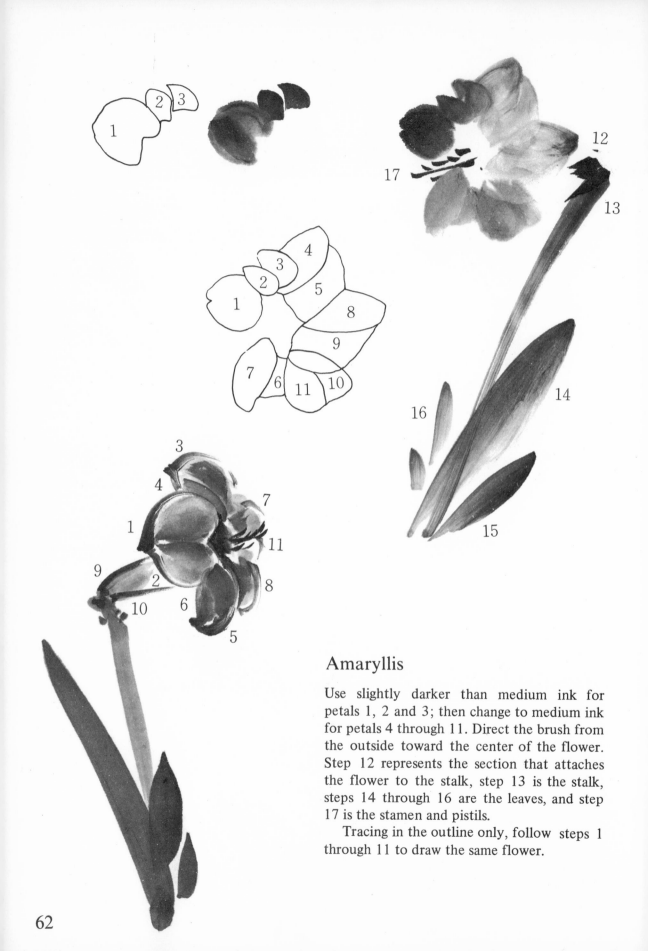

Amaryllis

Use slightly darker than medium ink for petals 1, 2 and 3; then change to medium ink for petals 4 through 11. Direct the brush from the outside toward the center of the flower. Step 12 represents the section that attaches the flower to the stalk, step 13 is the stalk, steps 14 through 16 are the leaves, and step 17 is the stamen and pistils.

Tracing in the outline only, follow steps 1 through 11 to draw the same flower.

Iris

Using medium ink with the tip dipped in dark ink and moving the brush downward, paint petals 1, 2 and 3. For petals 4 and 5, slant the brush and make downward strokes. Changing to a larger brush charged with medium ink and dark ink in the tip and working out from the center of the flower, paint 6 and 7 in strokes from right to left. For 8 and 9, stroke from left to right. With light ink, make the calyx; then move the brush downward for the stalk (10 and 11). For the leaves I have used the three-ink brush (12, 13, and 14) and dark ink only for 15, 16, and 17, but vary the colors as you like. The bud (18) painted with three-color ink and the veins in the petals are the finishing touches.

Stroke directions for painting an iris.

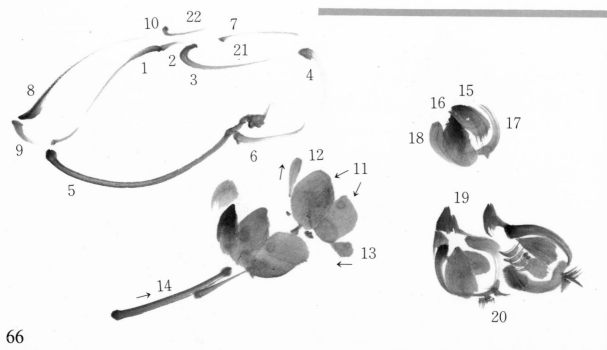

1 2 3 4 5 6 7 8 9 10 11 12 13 14 15 16 17 18 19 20 21 22

Wooden Shoes and Tulips

First outline the shoe in the front, then the one in the back. Next move on to the tulips, which should be painted in medium ink with a sharply slanted brush moving in the directions of the arrows. Use an upward stroke for the stalk. After painting 15 through 18 with medium ink, make the bud (19) with light ink. Finally, dip the tip of a brush charged with medium ink into dark ink. Press hard to make the shadows on the insides of the shoes (21 and 22).

Terse Outline Painting

Cat, Flower, Birds, and Rabbit

Said to have been originated by a priest named Toba (1053–1140), the *hakubyoho* or white painting method, that is, outlining and leaving the central space white, effectively expresses the natures of animals who move a great deal—birds, rabbits, cats,— and of half-opened flowers. Have the whole picture clearly drawn in your mind before you begin; you might even sketch in a pencil under-picture because once you have taken your brush in hand, there should be no stopping until the picture is complete.

After outlining the two birds with the *hakubyoho* method, I added light-ink shading.

69

The New Abstract Sumi-e

Cat

Sumi-e can be both extremely realistic and highly abstract; in fact, the abstract element of leaving large areas of white space in ink paintings has been a part of sumi-e for centuries. The cat, painted in a style I originated, reveals both the realistic and the abstract aspects of ink painting.

After charging a medium brush heavily with very dark ink, draw the top of the cat's head with one stroke (1), then the right and left ears with upward strokes (2). With two strokes of a fairly large brush, shape the forehead (3), and add the nose (4). To make the eyes easier to shape, paint a

few extra small brush strokes at 3 to achieve the right effect; then at 5 add the lines below the eyes. After painting the eyes, and the nose, complete the outline of the head in medium ink. At 7, starting slightly away from the face, add the whiskers, remembering to relax your fingers and wrist and to draw each line in a single quick stroke.

The body is easy to paint if you think of it in terms of divisions A, B, and C. These three strokes are extremely important because the success of the cat's body depends on them.

The following three points are vital:

1. Proper balance between the head and the body.
2. Clarity of the lines in the body.
3. A, B, and C must be one line each. No corrections are possible.
4. Much practice is needed to paint this picture well.

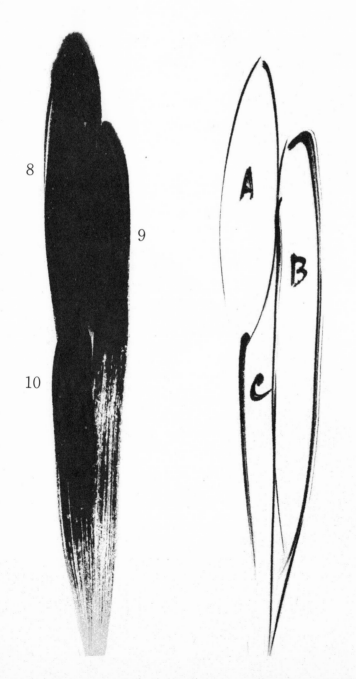

8

9

10

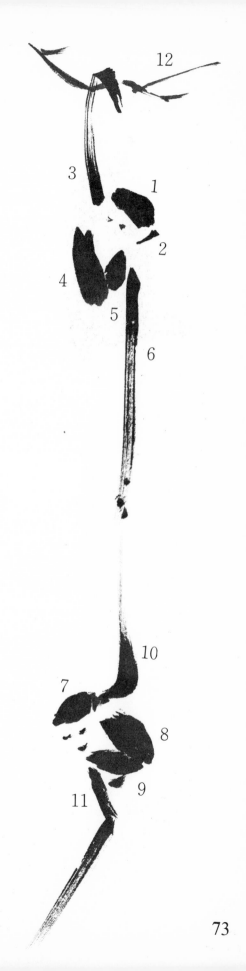

Monkeys

Strokes 1 through 6 complete the top monkey, and 7 through 11, the bottom monkey. At 12, add the branch from which they are swinging.

73

Kitten

Using dark ink, first paint the left ear. After washing the brush and charging it with medium ink, paint the right ear· with a downward stroke. Charge the brush with dark ink again, and outline the right ear and the eyes (3). Paint the eyes and nose with light ink (4), the front and rear paws with dark ink (5 and 6), and then in one smooth stroke, the tail. Since the relationship between the ear and the tail determines the size of the kitten, establish it with care. Finally, using a small brush, add the whiskers in such a way as to suggest a round kittenish face.

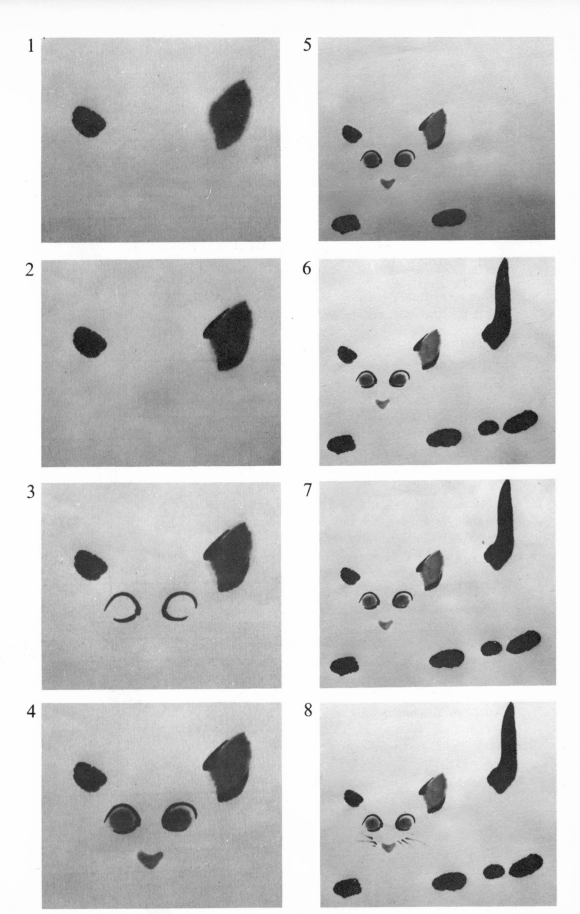

Subject Matter from Classical Chinese and Japanese Paintings

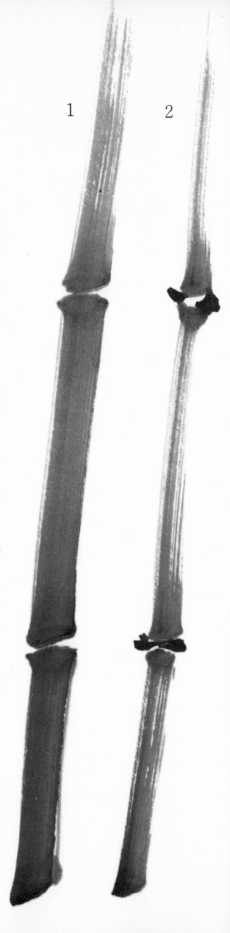

1   2

Bamboo

Ever since the Chinese Lady Li, in the period of the Five Dynasties (907–960), saw and appreciated the beauty of bamboo reflected on a window in the moonlight, similar representations of the plant have been important subjects for basic ink-painting training.

In the bamboo stalk in 1, be careful with the following points:

1. The brush is held at an angle.
2. The brush should be large.
3. Charge the brush in three-ink fashion by dipping it first in water, next in medium ink to half its length, finally only the tip in dark ink.
4. Brush stroke order is from the bottom to top.
5. A standard sumi-e bamboo stalk consists of three or five sections.
6. The sections should be longer at the top of the stalk, and the last section should be unfinished.
7. Since it is necessary to paint the entire stalk without recharging the brush, estimate how much ink you will need from the very beginning.
8. Starting at the bottom of the stalk, first press the brush against the paper. Paint upward, and press the brush again at the end of the section. Do not press the brush at the end of the last section of the stalk. The sections should be just the right distance apart: not open too wide, not too close together.

To paint the section divisions, first draw the modified version of the Chinese character *pi*, which means must, in the lowest opening (3A). Continue up the stalk by adding the remaining characters in modified forms: *shin* (the heart), *i* (the second, the latter), *i* (one), *ha* (eight).

The method for painting small branches, shown in 4, is called deer antlers.

Fig. 5 shows a slightly more complicated, though still basic, method of painting small branches; the method is called fishbones because the branches are arranged right and left of the main stalk.

3

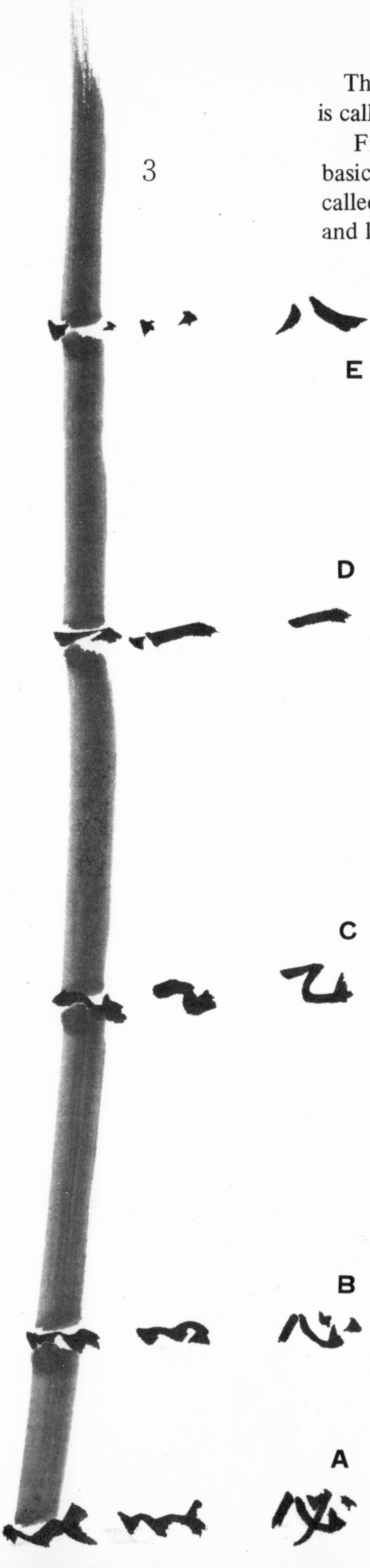

E

D

C

B

A

4

5

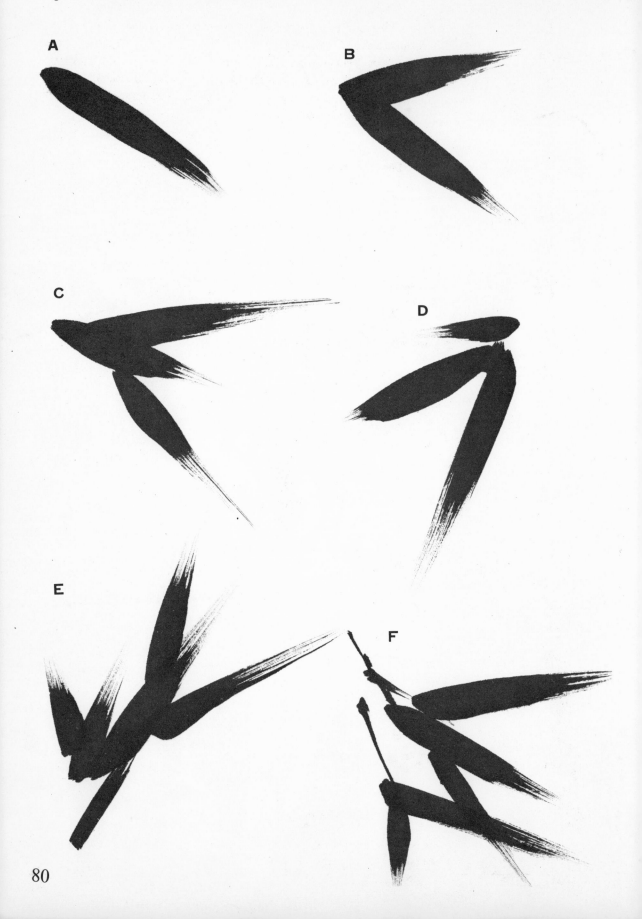

A

B

C

D

E

F

Painting bamboo leaves with single strokes suggesting the shape of a fish body is explained in Fig. 6. A is the basic single-stroke method; B, a two-stroke method, is called fishtail because the two leaves, neither too close together nor too far apart, should meet just as the two halves of a fish's tail. In painting the version in C thinking of a goldfish tail helps beginners. Fig. 6 D is another version with three leaves; in such groups all the leaves should start from different points. The leaves in E use upward strokes and are a composition of the grouping in B and that in C. F is an inverted version of E.

The people of the Orient have developed many ways of painting the leaves of the bamboo because in its strength against driving rains and its ability to bend to the winds without breaking, they see a symbol of their own way of life. Fig. 7A shows rain-drenched bamboo, whereas B represents bamboo in a gusty wind.

7 A

B

81

8

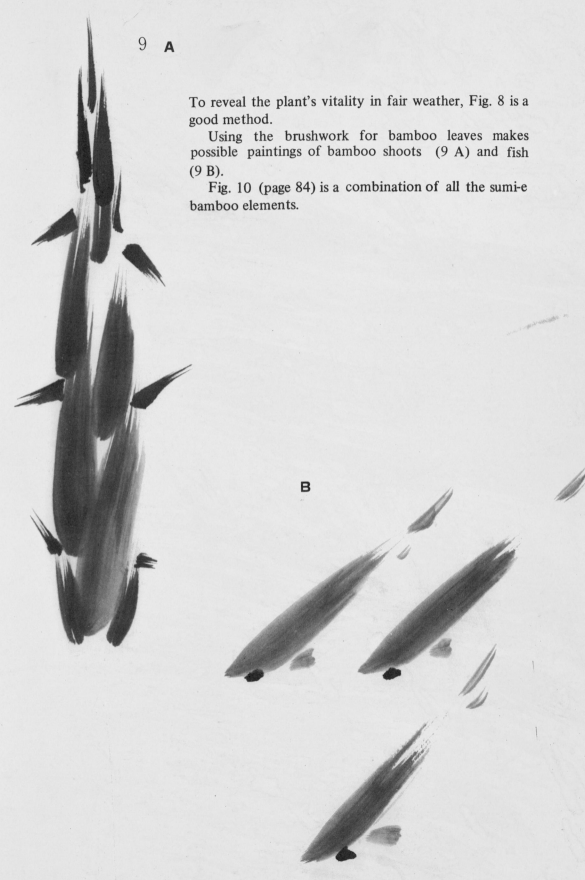

9 **A**

To reveal the plant's vitality in fair weather, Fig. 8 is a good method.

Using the brushwork for bamboo leaves makes possible paintings of bamboo shoots (9 A) and fish (9 B).

Fig. 10 (page 84) is a combination of all the sumi-e bamboo elements.

B

Mountains

After first outlining the mountains (strokes 1 through 9), suggest the tree coverage with light-ink horizontal strokes (10) and with occasional dots of dark-ink to hint at luxuriance.

A

1 2 3 4 5 6

Boulders

Instead of the usual method of having students practice painting boulders in original landscapes, I include two stones that should be of assistance. In the outline of the boulder in Fig. A, it is important to press the brush into the paper from time to time to give the feeling of a rough surface.

The boulder in Fig. B uses much the same brushwork to achieve the impression of a flat, smooth stone.

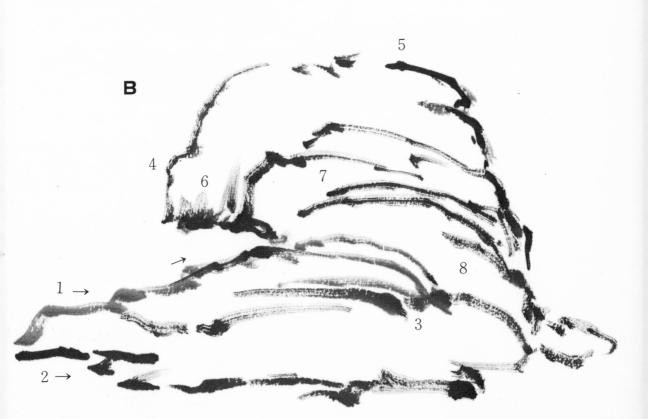

C

Use light ink in the shaded areas, and the brighter
places will naturally stand out. Adding spots of dark ink
here and there increases the richness of the texture.

D

89

1  2

4

5

6

3

Boulder and Bamboo Grass

After painting a part of the boulder in medium ink, following the direction shown by the arrows in 1, complete the shape, and shade the stone (steps 2 through 5). With a fine brush and dark ink, paint part of the bamboo grass to face left (6) and part to face right (7). Complete the composition with a small stone and some grass. (Note: combining steps 6 and 7 produces a bamboo tree.)

7

Other Long-popular Flowers

Chrysanthemums

The aster in Fig. A—asters belong to the chrysanthemum family—should be made by painting the petals first using medium ink. Working the brush from the periphery inward avoid exact symmetrical placements. Add dark-ink dots for the center of the flower.

Gradually working from the center outward in the directions indicated by the arrows in B, complete the chrysanthemum in C.

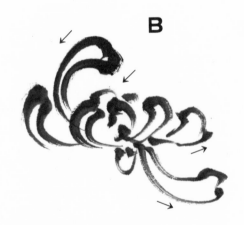

C

Wild Orchids

Using medium ink, begin first with the long orchid leaves (1–6); to paint the full-open and semi-open blossoms, refer to the following examples. The full flower has five petals, painted in light ink, and a dark trumpet; the stem should be light. Paint from the outside inward.

One of the so-called "four gentlemanly plants"(plum, chrysanthemum, orchid, and bamboo), the orchid has long been important sumi-e training material because it helps develop a quick, light, smooth, and gentle brush technique. Often growing in high, well-aired places and frequently requiring no soil at all, the orchid is compared to the gentleman who needs no estate to preserve his gentility. Consequently, to paint it best, one must divest himself of worldy thoughts and become spiritually much like the orchid.

Quince on the Bough

For the quince, which in the Orient blooms as the plum, use the three-ink method to achieve a gently modulated tonal effect. Begin with area 1 of the large branch; then add area 2 and the small branch (3). After adding two or three blossoms (4), use dark ink for their centers (5), and finally dark ink dots to suggest the rough texture of the bark (6).

Quince Blossoms

The varieties and parts of the blossom are as follows: (1) the full bud, (2) the calyx, (3) the open flower, (4) a semi-side view of the flower, (5) full-open flower with pistil and stamens, and (6) tightly closed bud. Fig. 7 shows how to paint the leaves: use medium ink, and add the veins after the leaves have dried. Young leaves are painted as shown in Fig. 8.

Plum Blossoms

Figs. 1–7 show plum buds and blossoms that, when gracefully combined, make the branches of flowers shown above. The shapes of the petals and the sharp spiny appearance of the young branches are important.

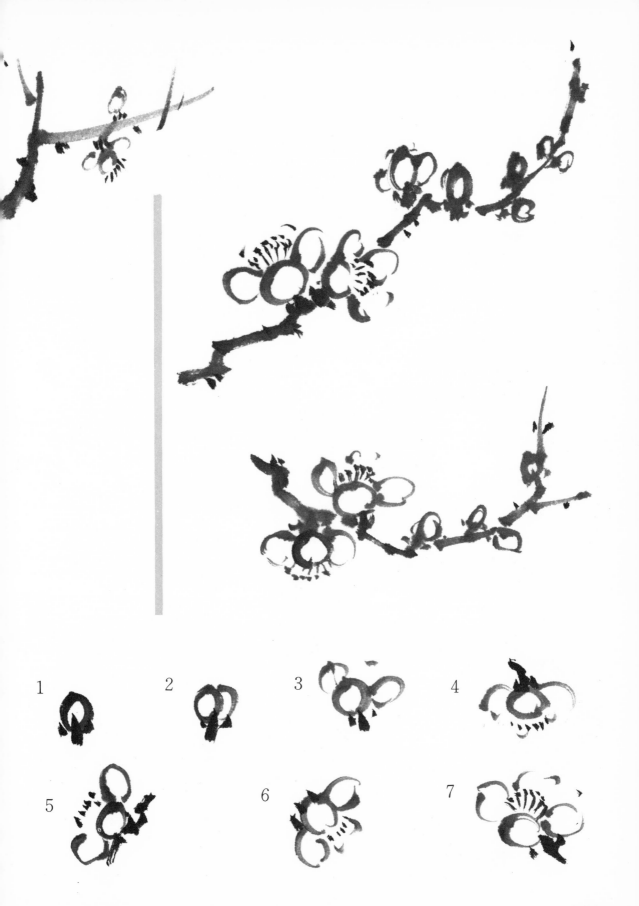

1

2

3

4

5

6

7

Some Interesting Combinations

Teapot

Using dark ink and a medium brush, begin with the lid
(1), then the sockets for the handle (2), the spout (3),
the general shape (4), and the handle (5). Finally, add
the cups; then changing to a large brush charged with
medium ink, shade as indicated.

1

2

3

6

4

7

5

8

Bird's Nest in a Broken Teapot

Following the explanations already given, use dark ink for the bird and medium and light for everything else. The dried grass in the hole in the pot should suggest a bird's nest.

Easter Basket

Figs. A, B, C, D, and E indicate the proper ways to paint and shade the full-blooming and half-open lilies. The basket, eggs, and leaves should be painted as shown in F.

Paint the flowers first, then add a section of the basket so that the lilies appear in the middle. Next, following the numbers, add a chick and the easter eggs. After adding a few blades of grass, sketch in a section of the handle, and, with light ink, color the eggs and the basket. Showing only parts of the basket and handle sets the chick off to better advantage.

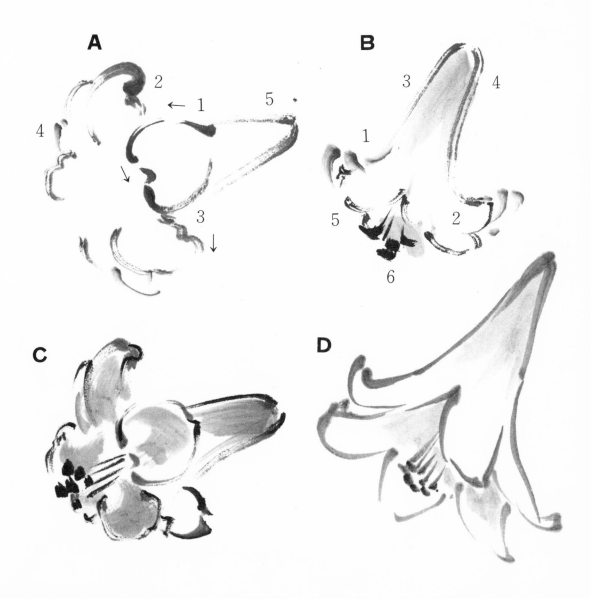

E

F

Fish that Seem to Swim

Game Fish

After painting the eye and head (1 and 2), dip a large brush in water, medium ink, and dark ink–just the tip– and in a single stroke toward the tail, paint the fish body. Add the gill plate (3), the fins (4, 5, 6, and 7), and finally the tail. The line of the tail must flow from the body to give the impression of the fish's motion through the water.

Goldfish

Paint the eye and head with dark ink (1 and 2); then with light ink add the tail and dorsal fins (3 and 4). After adding the lower fins and the outline of the belly (5), using a small brush and dark ink, suggest scales, and add the fine veins to the fins and tail. Suggest the fish's habitat by adding water grass.

5

6

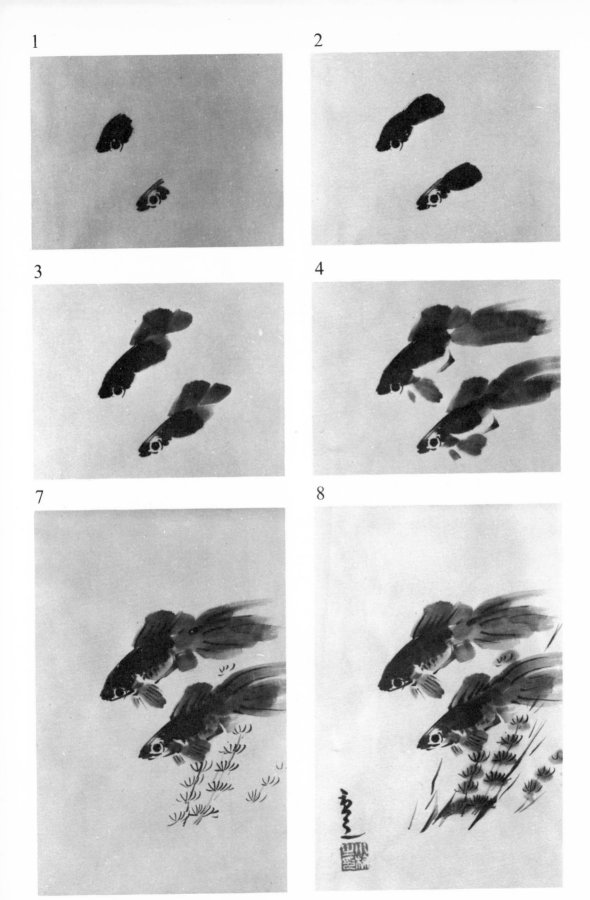

Fisherman

Painting the human figure is much the same in the East and West.

   To achieve a smooth line for the fishing pole, dip the tip of a fine brush in dark ink, hold the brush by the base (near the bristles), put the tip of the little finger on the paper, and draw the line following the little finger.

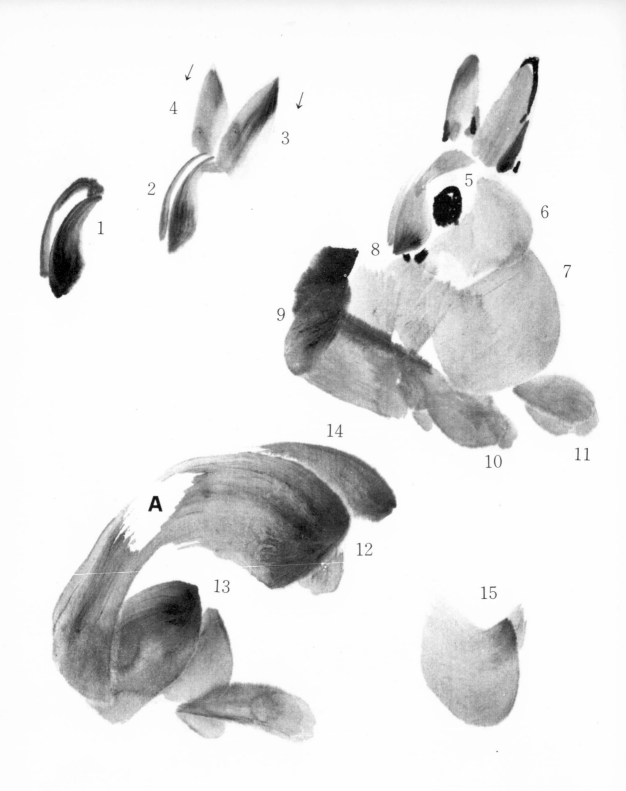

Suggesting Strength with Heavy Lines

Rabbit

Using medium ink and moving the brush downward, paint the face and ears (1–4), and with dark ink add the eye. Light ink strokes 6, 7, and 8 represent the chin and breast, whereas dark ink in 9, 10, and 11, produces the legs. Changing to a larger brush, paint the rear section (12, 13, and 14); do not be concerned if some places are uninked as in A. Wash the brush, and with dark ink add the rounded tail, and finally correct the shape of the ears.

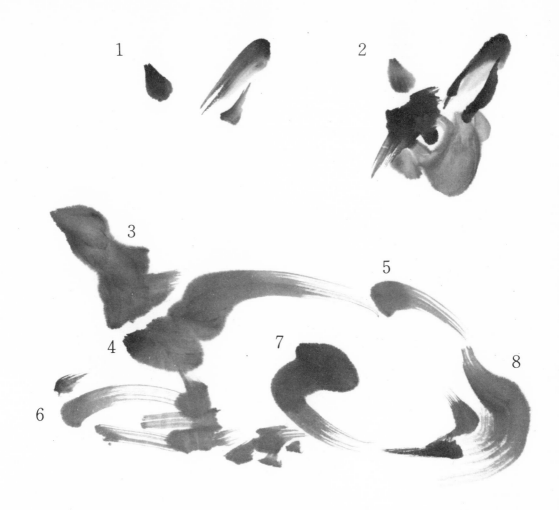

Donkey

To paint the symbol of the American Democratic Party, begin with the ears, then the head, neck, and chest; and follow in the numerical order shown in the picture. Unless the ears are long and the nose and the white patch above it are carefully rendered, the picture may look like a horse. Use dark lines for the outline of the ears and light for the chest, upper back, and legs.

Striped Squirrel

The painting method is the same as that for a tree-climbing squirrel except that it is necessary to leave space between lines to indicate stripes. Nonarboreal, this squirrel should be pictured in grass on the ground instead of on a tree branch.

Elephant

To draw the Republican Party symbol, paint the elephant so as to suggest purposeful forward motion. Stroke 9 should outline a full rounded belly. Once the outline is completed, use medium and light ink to shade.

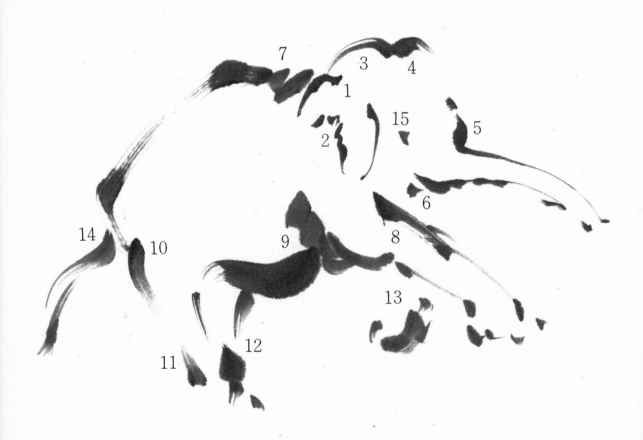